SNOOP
A Spiritual Memoir Of A Vietnam Army Grunt

I Am A Soldier Of Jesus Christ

Dr. C. Wayne Harrison
"Snoopy"

PUBLISHED *by* PARABLES
Earthly Stories with a Heavenly Meaning

Snoopy: A Spiritual Memoir Of A Vietnam Army Grunt
Am A Soldier Of Jesus Christ
Copyright © Dr. C. Wayne Harrison
Published By Parables

Unless otherwise specified Scripture quotations are taken from the authorized version of the Neew King James Bible.

First Edition   March, 2016

ISBN 978-0-9966165-8-4

Printed in the United States of America

Readers should be aware that Internet Web sites offered as citations and/or sources for further information may have been changed or disappeared between the time this was written and when it is read.

Illustration provided by www.unsplash.com

From The Book

When the fighting stopped, there was that silent reminder that someone's hope had been taken away. Hope lost and gone forever.

Strange as it seems to me now, I cannot remember ever thinking about the eternal destination of any of those enemy soldiers we faced in battle. They were the enemy and it was our job to kill them, and that is what we did.

The days were long, hot, and very difficult, even if you did not make contact with the enemy. Just being a jungle fighter, with all you own and all you need to survive on your back, made each day so miserable, that there were times when you almost wished to die to put an end to the difficulties of the moment.

The truth of the matter is, whether in civilian life or the life of a soldier, we need one another to be successful, to be assured of winning the victory.

...there is something about a soldier that will cause him to act in a way that would not seem normal to others. There is that desire to do well, but it's more than just doing well, more than just being successful, more than just winning, more than just living. A real soldier wants to fight with honor, whether in living or dying, to fight with honor.

Howard and I made eye contact for just a moment. We didn't speak. There was just that look affirming that death was certain. We opened fire, never letting up on the trigger. I would kill until my ammo was spent and then I would die.

Arriving home, back to the United States of America, does not end the hurt. You would think that to return home alive would put an end to all the hurt, all the pain.....you would think. Unfortunately this is not true. No war has been as unsupported as the Vietnam war, and no soldiers have been so disrespected as the Vietnam veterans. Coming home was not an end to the hurt, but rather a new hurt, one even more painful than hot shrapnel burning into your body.

ACKNOWLEDGEMENTSS

This book is only made possible by the leadership
Of my Lord and Savior, Jesus Christ. I am thankful for His
leadership and the gift of recall for these special events in my life.
This book would not be a reality without the encouragement of my wife,
Glenda, who continued to remind me of the need to complete this work as
God had directed. Also for our children, Jody and his wife Kerri, for Amy
and her husband Brett, and our six sweet grandchildren, Halle Kate,
Bailey, Kenlee Elizabeth, Nathan, Karsyn Fayth, and little Jonah,
I love these blessings with all of my heart.

SNOOP
A Spiritual Memoir Of A
Vietnam Army Grunt

I Am A Soldier Of Jesus Christ

Dr. C. Wayne Harrison
"Snoopy"

PUBLISHED *by* PARABLES
Earthly Stories with a Heavenly Meaning

TABLE OF CONTENTS

Dedication

These pages share just some of the many challenges of a combat soldier in any battle. My war was Vietnam where I served as a jungle fighter with two combat units. The first was with Bravo Company 2/16th 1st Infantry Division, and the second was with Charlie Company 3/187th 101st Airborne Division. Almost fifty-nine thousand men and women gave their lives fighting to maintain freedom for those being oppressed by those communist aggressors. Thousands more have and are feeling the effects of this war even today. These pages and these stories are dedicated to these who sacrificed all. They are the real heroes of Vietnam. Thank you all for your gift to preserve the freedom we enjoy and so often take for granted in this great country, the United States of America.

ABOUT THE AUTHOR

Dr. Chester Wayne Harrison is the pastor of East Prentiss Baptist Church and founder of REACHING MINISTRY, taking the Gospel to the world through mission adventures. He has been married for forty-seven years to Glenda. They have two children and six grandchildren. His military experience took him to the jungles of Vietnam where he served deeply embedded as a guerrilla soldier, hunting and being hunted. Life is a journey and the challenges we face each day mold and make us, preparing us for the next day. My motto: If you live to fight another day, it's been a good day. May God's richest blessings be yours as you read this book and share it with others.

DR. C. WAYNE HARRISON

"You therefore, my son, be strong in the grace that is in Christ Jesus. And the things that you have heard from me among many witnesses, commit these to faithful men who will be able to teach others also. You therefore must endure hardship as a good soldier of Jesus Christ. No one engaged in warfare entangles himself with the affairs of this life, that he may please Him who enlisted him as a soldier."

-- II Timothy 2: 1-4 NKJV

PHOTOGRAPHY INDEX

Chapter 1
The Heart
Of A Soldier

"You therefore, my son, be strong in the grace that is in Christ Jesus. And the things that you have heard from me among many witnesses, commit these to faithful men who will be able to teach others also. You therefore must endure hardship as a good soldier of Jesus Christ. No one engaged in warfare entangles himself with the affairs of this life, that he may please Him who enlisted him as a soldier."
-- II Timothy 2: 1-4 NKJV

The evening dew glistened on the leaves of the thick vegetation all around me. Darkness had overtaken the light of day. The dampness of the night made it easier for me to slither through the grass like a snake, unnoticed. My mission was simple: take out an observation position without drawing the attention of the other enemy soldiers camped fifty meters away.

As quietly as I could I crawled, making my way closer and closer to the unsuspecting enemy. The sharp blades of the elephant grass sliced my arms and the sweat made them sting. The bugs of the night were feasting on me. But I could not afford to slap my face to kill them for fear of giving away my position.

I was close and drawing closer. I could see the light from their fire casting shadows. I could smell the spices from their meager meal, mostly rice. I could even see the darkness in the eyes of the soldier who sat across from his two comrades.

Wait a minute, I was not expecting three soldiers, only two. This would change my tactics and make my mission more difficult. None of the three suspected that I was so near, or that death was nearer still.

I had rehearsed in my mind exactly how I would attack, who I would kill first, then second, and last. Everything had to be perfect. The slightest miscue would alert their fellow soldiers and cost a greater loss of life of my fellow soldiers. As dusk was turning to deep darkness, I knew it was time for a surprise attack, one that would leave my foe lying in death. My rifle in one hand and my knife in the other, I positioned myself so I could spring quickly, like a lion on his prey.

I was just about to pounce when the silence of the night was broken with a shrilling cry that made the hair on my neck stand aright. "Chester Wayne, Chester Wayne, it is time to come in and get ready for bed". It was the call of my mother, calling me to come inside, because it was getting too late to play outside. I was quickly brought back to reality. I was not a soldier in a jungle on a foreign land, but just a boy in northeast Mississippi, pretending to fight a battle for my country. Little did I know, even at this early age, God had placed in my chest the heart of a soldier that one day would live out these imaginations in the jungles of Vietnam.

God, who is the Creator of all things, and the Giver of all life, places within each of us the potential to be His faithful soldier. This I know to be true, because on August 28, 1950, God placed the heart of a soldier in a little boy born to a simple, rural Mississippi couple, Chester and Vernice Harrison. As long as I can remember, the desire to be a soldier has been burning in my heart.

My Dad was a tail gunner on a B-24 with the Eighth Air Force stationed in England. He made bombing raids over Germany during World War II until Germany surrendered. My ancestors have been involved in every war to protect and secure our freedom in this great land all the way back to the American Revolution. It is consistent with my heritage that I would have a heart-felt longing to be a soldier.

Playing in the hills and valleys of northeast Mississippi during those growing up years, my imagination allowed me to fight in every war that our history books have recorded. Just as those timeless pages described, victory after victory came with each battle as I fought courageously in my young mind. Still there was a greater desire to do more than just "pretend", I wanted more than anything else to be a soldier.

Growing up during the Cold War, I had prepared myself for an invasion by Russia and was ready to cause havoc in their ranks with my trusty rifle and guerrilla tactics. Even these times of play prepared me for the savvy necessary to fight and survive in the jungles of Southeast Asia. The foolishness of a young mind allowed me to dream big dreams not realizing that God had designed a purpose for my life that would make many of those dreams come true.

As my teenage years came my thoughts turned to sports and the desire to excel as a player on the ball field. You see, my Dad had been a great baseball player and had signed a contract with the Memphis Chicks after his military obligations had been met. I wanted to be like my Dad in every way, and so I determinedly focused on being the best athlete I could possibly be. Even in sports the heart of a soldier yielded the fruit of strength and desire that made possible the developed ability to excel.

Not all battles are immediately seen as victories. Sometimes we find ourselves seemingly defeated only to discover later that a greater victory had been won. These greater victories produce even greater joy and greater courage to face the trials of battle that would most certainly come on a different field of valor. Only our Commander in Chief, Jesus can know the outcome of each field of battle on which we find ourselves engaging a vicious enemy. As good soldiers of our Lord, we must be true to our life calling and fight diligently until the battle is over.

During my sophomore year in high school I played football on the "B" team, or the junior varsity team. Being the smallest player on the team made it difficult for me to get much playing time. My greatest ability was in catching the football and this I could do with great confidence, but the problem was our team did not throw many passes. We were a run oriented team, and when we did pass, it was to one of the larger and older players on the team.

Still, there was no quit in my heart. I wanted to play, and I was determined to do my best to gain the attention of the coaches on our team. But try as I did, the only playing time I got was on special teams and late in the games that had already been decided. This was not what I had dreamed of, but I practiced hard, obeyed my coaches, and accepted the limited time on the field during the game.

The most memorable catch I made was in Tupelo, Mississippi on a cold rainy Thursday night during pregame drills as we prepared for our arch rivals, the Golden Wave. Knowing that passing would be out of the question, still we went through our warm up passing drills. During the "ten and out" our quarterback Bobby Morris threw a pass that slipped from his hand and came very low, only about ten inches off of the ground. Without breaking a stride I caught that pass, and this was before tacky gloves and sticky substances sometimes used today. Did our coaches notice that catch? I could only hope my sure hands would gain me time on the field of battle, but as the game progressed, just as in ever other game, my only playing time came on special teams.

To receive a football letter, you had to play in a certain amount of quarters during the season. Each player kept up with his quarters, as did I. With one game left to play, I only needed one quarter to earn my letter, but played in three quarters, thus assuring that a big black "C" letter would be mine.

I had worked hard that summer mowing yards and other odd jobs to save up enough money to buy that white sweater with the black ring around the sleeve which identified you as a football player at Corinth High School. The trip to town to Bigger's Hardware and Sporting Goods to buy that sweater was a day of great joy. Even though I did not have enough money to buy it that day, I put it in the layaway and in a few more weeks had earned enough money to pay my debt and get my sweater.

My Mom sewed my number on the sleeve, and now I was all set to show off my new Corinth Warrior sweater at school. After wearing it to school a couple of times, my girlfriend, Glenda became the proud owner of the sweater until the day our football letters were presented at school. That day I would wear with pride that symbol of a football player, a Corinth High School Warrior.

We assembled in the gym for the presentation of awards and letters. Coach Ray Long our Athletic Director stood to speak about the good year in football for the varsity and the junior varsity teams. Near the end of his speech he told us that not all players who had earned a letter would be receiving one this year. My heart began to melt, my mind began to wonder, and these questions stirred my heart. Would I get a letter, what about my sweater, and what would all my friends think?

The names were called, and every player on our team who had earned a letter received a letter except me. It seemed that all those on the team turned and looked at me, as though they couldn't believe it. Many looked at me with pity in their eyes. I was crushed. I had worked so hard. I had given it my very best. This was not fair, but I walked away, took off that sweater, removed the numbers on the sleeve, and put it in the closet in my room. I never wore that sweater again. It still hangs in my closet fifty years and counting, serving as a reminder of the disappointment that can be experienced on the field of battle.

Some lessons are learned with much pain, and all battles require a willingness to make any sacrifice necessary to win the victory. Paul knew this to be true by personal experience, for he found himself imprisoned, beaten, and stoned many times during his walk with the Lord and for the Lord in his many battles of sharing the Gospel. Difficult tasks and seemingly unfair events are used by our Lord to prepare us for the greater battles that are before us. This lesson would be remembered later in the jungles of Vietnam, and in the spiritual battles in which I would be engaged as a pastor of God's children. If we are to stand for Christ at any cost the motto of the First Infantry Division, the Big Red One, "No Mission Too Difficult, No Sacrifice Too Great" must echo through the corridors of our heart. When facing the enemy in battle, like Timothy, we must "endure hardship as a good soldier of Jesus Christ", and this requires the heart of a soldier.

From One Soldier To Another

1. What is the deep down, earnest desire of your heart? What is it that you long for more than anything else?

2. Does your strength come from the grace of our Lord, Jesus Christ, or from some other source?

3. What entanglements prevents you from engaging boldly in the hardship of the spiritual warfare of our Lord?

A Soldier's Prayer

Dear Heavenly Father, the God of all creation, I magnify Your holy name, and seek Your listening ear. Free me from the entanglements of this life, and free me so that I may successfully engage in the spiritual battles that are yet before me. With Your help I desire to have the heart of a soldier of Jesus Christ. In the name of Jesus, I pray. Amen.

CHAPTER 2
THE HANDS
OF A SOLDIER

"Live joyfully with the wife whom you love all the days of your vain life which He has given you under the sun, all of your days of vanity; for that is your portion in life, and in the labor which you perform under the sun. Whatever your hand finds to do, do it with your might; for there is no work or device or knowledge or wisdom in the grave where you are going."
-- Ecclesiastes 9: 9-10 NKJV

Football was not going to be a part of my future, so my efforts turned to baseball, and after all, it was as a second baseman that my Dad was noticed by the Memphis Chicks who signed him to play for them. My last two years of high school baseball were very rewarding, yet frustrating, as again I found myself not given the opportunity to prove myself as I knew I could on the field of play. Still I practiced and played hard, and I did earn a letter for my varsity jacket my junior and senior years. However, two knee injuries, one which cost me a tryout with the St. Louis Cardinals, and graduation from high school made me realize that professional sports was not going to be my way of life. Again it would seem that I had been defeated on life's battlefield.

During a revival meeting, when I was nine years old, I asked God to forgive me of my sins. I invited Jesus Christ to come into my heart and be my Lord and Savior. Even so, Jesus had not yet become the focus of my life. I attended church every time the doors were open, but I was not growing as God intended. This caused much of my frustration during my high school years.

The brightest spot of those teenage years was getting to know and falling in love with Glenda Rider. I was so bashful and backwards, but since God had made her just for me, it was only a matter of time until each of us would realize that God was bringing us together. After graduation we were married, and the beginning of new challenges and new battles began. After forty seven years and counting, each day I find myself facing the enemy that would destroy that which God has so graciously put together.

Marriage is hard work. It requires each person giving their all each and every day to survive the evil assaults made by our enemy, Satan. We were committed to make our home safe and one where love always prevails. Everything that we knew to do, we did, because we did not want to be another married couple struggling to make love last. What a great time we had learning more and more about each other every day.

Looking back on those early months of our marriage, following our honeymoon at Buzzard Roost, Glenda and I set lofty goals for our marriage. At Pickwick Lakes, I see two young people working hard at becoming what God expects of a husband and wife. My Dad had taught me to always do my best in everything, just as God's Word says, "Whatever your hand finds to do, do it with all your might".

The greatest challenge of our first year of marriage came when I volunteered for the Army. The heart of a soldier and the desire to serve my country in Vietnam called on each of us to reach into the depth of our souls for God's strength and courage to face the days that were ahead of us. I did not realize just how difficult this would make life for my dear little wife, but looking back and beginning to understand as best I can, I know that she displayed the heart of a soldier, a soldier's wife. On that cool spring morning, I kissed my wife goodbye before leaving to become that soldier, fulfilling the desire that God had placed in my heart as a child.

The morning of April 2, 1969 the group leaving from the Corinth bus station was all present and ready to travel. Some were not as anxious for the adventure that lay ahead as I was. The responsibility of the paperwork for everyone on the bus was placed in my care. Right away I am given a small amount of respect and responsibility that I had never received from anyone else except my wife, Glenda.

God was about to do something very special in my life to mold and make me in His fashion and He would use the United States Army to get the job done. God has a plan for each life, and if we will just patiently wait and watch He will develop a character in each child of God that will example one who possesses the heart of a soldier.

When we arrived at the Army Reception Station in Memphis later that morning, the pace became quicker, much quicker. The Army was now in charge and it would seem that everything they told us to do was to be done with a sense of urgency. After what seemed to be a brief physical examination, I found myself in a crowded room with my right hand raised, and taking an oath that still has an important place in my heart. The words of this vow are simple but carry a great responsibility. They are.... "I do solemnly swear that I will support and defend the Constitution of the United States against all enemies, foreign and domestic; that I will bear true faith and allegiance to the same; and that I will obey the orders of the president of the United States and the orders of the officers appointed over me, according to regulations and the Uniform Code of Military Justice. So help me God."

In the words of that vow I was simply promising to my country and my God that I would conduct myself as one who has the heart of a soldier. With pride I worded that vow, and I knew that from that moment on I was a soldier, a dream come true.

A cold box lunch, a long bus ride, and then later that night I arrived at Fort Campbell, Kentucky, home of the 101st Airborne Division and my home for the next several weeks of basic training. What can I say about basic training except that it was a time of discipline and training, and more discipline and training, with time to get a "buzz" haircut each Friday whether you needed it or not. This was a time that the Army used to get soldiers into shape by breaking away those things that are really not necessary in our lives, and breaking you down so they could build up a soldier. However, God used this time to remold my heart and mind, and without me even knowing it, He was getting me ready to serve as a soldier of my Savior.

I was eighteen years old. Some would say I was just a boy, but I like to think I was a man, and I knew I was developing into something that I had never imagined in those younger years of yearning to be a soldier. I wasn't the best soldier in our company, but I did well, well enough to get a stripe before leaving basic, and the opportunity to qualify with the M-16 rifle.

The M-16 was the weapon of choice in Vietnam, and this early introduction to this weapon assured me that my longing to serve in combat was getting closer. After those difficult weeks of basic training, and marching on the parade field on the day of graduation, once again I found myself kissing Glenda "goodbye", because no leave or weekend pass was granted. It seemed the war in Southeast Asia was in a hurry for our arrival. So once again I boarded a bus, this time for Fort Polk, Louisiana. As we entered the camp in the early morning hours, above the entrance were written these words, "We Train Men for Vietnam".

Advanced Infantry Training, or A.I.T. was a time of final stateside preparation for a war that many did not understand, and one that still causes pain for so many today. Here I was equipped with knowledge about tactics and survival in a combat situation, and especially trained for jungle warfare. I was becoming a "grunt", the affectionate name for the foot soldier whose job it is to do the difficult and dirty work in unfriendly and hostile surroundings. After weeks of rigorous conditioning and training, the time of preparation was about to escalate. No matter how much you study and prepare, the final training and the final test are taken on the fields of battle, or in my case, the jungles of Vietnam.

Once again I found myself on a parade field, having earned another stripe, and with orders for my next assignment, the First Infantry Division, The Big Red One, which was serving in the Central Highlands of South Vietnam. The joy of completion of this phase of my military life was magnified by the presence of my sweet little wife, who had traveled a long way for this ceremony. With only a few days leave before departure for Vietnam, Glenda and I were determined to make the most of this time together. Now she had a different man by her side, from now on I would always hold her with the hands of a soldier.

FROM ONE SOLDIER TO ANOTHER

1.   Look at your hands. Whose hands do you see, yours or God's?

2.   Look at your hands. These hands are made for life, for love, and for labor. Do your hands honor God in each of these areas?

3.   Look at your hands. Will you commit these hands with all of your might to serve your Savior and Lord?

A SOLDIER'S PRAYER

My gracious Father in heaven, You know all things and see all things, please hear my humble prayer. I willingly submit my hands to You, and ask for Your strength, that my labors might be acceptable in Your sight. With the heart of a soldier and the hands of a soldier I pledge my allegiance to You. In the name of Jesus, I pray. Amen.

CHAPTER 3
THE HARDSHIPS
OF A SOLDIER

"The people who walked in darkness have seen a great Light; those who dwell in the land of the shadow of death, upon them a Light has shined. You have multiplied the nation and increased its joy; they rejoice before You according to the joy of harvest, as men rejoice when they divide the spoil. For You have broken the yoke of his burden and the staff of his shoulder, the rod of his oppressor, as in the day of Midian. For every warrior's sandal from the noisy battle, and garments rolled in blood, will be used for burning and fuel of fire. For unto us a Child is born, unto us a Son is given; and the government shall be upon His shoulder. And His name will be called Wonderful Counselor, Mighty God, Everlasting Father, Prince of Peace. Of the increase of His government and peace there will be no end, upon the throne of David and over His kingdom, to order it and establish it with judgment and justice from that time forward, even forever. The zeal of the Lord of hosts will perform this." -- Isaiah 9: 2-7 NKJV

After a few days of leave that passed so quickly, around midnight on a warm August night, I kissed Glenda "goodbye" again, boarding an airplane whose final destination was Vietnam. The emotions that raced through my heart as we lifted from the runway grew even faster as I looked out the window and saw my precious wife weeping from the observation deck of the airport. This parting could be forever, and each of us knew this. The darkness overcame the lights of Memphis as we gained altitude and miles separated me from the person I loved most in just a matter of moments. The real hardships of being a soldier were not in all the intense training, but in the separation from the one you love.

The next few days in Oakland, California were very confusing and upsetting. Having dealt with the difficult departure from Glenda only hours earlier, now my orders for Vietnam were put on hold, and there were rumors that we were going to Germany. This possibility was good news for Glenda, but before much time for celebration, my orders were changed again for the final time.

Some of our group was going to Germany, but I would leave for "Nam" in just a couple of days. Several conversations with Glenda on the telephone only made these hours a time of hardship for each of us, saying "goodbye" over and over again. Suddenly, and with no time to call and talk to Glenda, I boarded a Flying Tiger Airline with one stop in Anchorage, Alaska, where I managed a two-minute call for one last time to tell Glenda "I love You", then one stop in Tokyo, Japan before arriving at our final destination, Saigon, South Vietnam.

There were almost three hundred soldiers on this flight, and while most of them slept, I could not. My heart's desire to be a combat soldier was coming true, but leaving my wife in tears and the horrors of the unknown were tearing into the fabric of my soul. Eleven Bravo was my M.O.S., my job description, which meant I was a foot soldier, or in this case, a jungle fighter. There would be no turning back now; the days of battle were quickly approaching.

Twenty six hours later we were making our final approach for landing when the pilot announced the date, the temperature, and the weather conditions. It was August 28, 1969, it was 151 degrees, and pouring down rain; it was my nineteenth birthday. This was a birthday that had completely gone unnoticed until that moment. The reality of where I was grasped my heart, and I could only wonder what was in the heart of my true love, Glenda.

Hardships come in many different ways for a soldier, even from your comrades in arms. As we walked across the runway in the pouring rain, under a shed only a few meters away stood almost three hundred soldiers waiting to board the same plane we had just walked away from, except they were going home, back to the "real world" as referred to by soldiers. I remember well as we walked drenched in the pouring rain the cries from under that shed of weary but happy soldiers, of "short, short, short".

"Short-timer" was what all soldiers looked forward to saying, because that meant that your time in the Nam was nearly over. For me, I knew my days there were many, and yet I could not help but wonder, if I would even live to stand under that shed when my days were up, or would my time be up sooner as the result of an enemy bullet? The hardships of being a solder were just beginning, there were even harder days before me, and before my dear wife, Glenda.

A few days of "Snake School", which was a time of orientation and adaptation to the climate and violence which surrounded you, passed quickly. I arrived in the field with my unit by way of a re-supply helicopter, and just a few minutes later I was part of the point team, walking "slack", and providing cover for the point man. It was my job to help keep him alive, but I wondered whose job it was to keep me alive. The mind games you would play increased the hardships of being a soldier, but these thoughts were short lived, because we made contact with an enemy unit later that afternoon.

I do not remember how long this fire fight lasted, but it seemed to go on and on forever. This was the first time anyone had ever shot at me, with the intent to kill me, and this was a new emotion, one that causes a release of adrenaline that seems to take over both body and mind. I responded as a soldier who had been trained by the best in the world. I was an American soldier, and I was willing to die for my country, if that was what this day required.

On this day, I never even saw the enemy face to face,

but it was evident from which area the enemy was firing, and we directed as much fire power as we could on that "hot spot". Just to make certain that the enemy had been destroyed, artillery was called in, and removed any doubt. After a "sweeping" of the area, and a body count that I learned was very important, we took a moment to rest and gather our thoughts before moving out for our ambush spot of the night.

I remember well as Lt. Kennedy, our platoon leader, came up to me and said, "Congratulations, Harrison, you've earned your C.I.B. on your first day". Those initials represent the pride of being a "grunt", for the Combat Infantry Badge is something that I still wear with pride and joy, knowing it stands for my faithfulness to endure the hardships of a soldier in the engagement of the enemy.

Not every day included contact with an enemy unit, but every day did include the hardship of being a foot soldier in the jungles of Vietnam. We carried four days of water and rations, a poncho and liner, one claymore mine, two hand grenades, two smoke grenades, two trip flares, twenty one magazines of ammo, and a rifle, all of which weighed about one hundred thirty five pounds. The dampness of the rainy season and the misery of the dry season made each day a hardship, and if that wasn't enough, "Charlie", the pet name for the Viet Cong, the enemy, was out there somewhere waiting to kill you.

Cold "C" rations, that had stamped on the bottom of the can, 1944, and were left over from World War II, were our meals each day. You haven't lived until you reach in your ruck sack at 0400 hours feeling a large can and hoping it is fruit, only to find out when you opened it that you were about to enjoy cold beef, scalloped potatoes and gravy with about two inches of grease on the top. You don't throw it away; it is a meal, so you eat it, grease and all.

The Scriptures in Isaiah says, "every warrior's sandal from the noisy battle, and garments rolled in blood, will be used for burning and fuel of fire". These words speak of a time when the battle is ended, yet while the war rages even the small luxury of sleeping with your boots off is far from reach on an ambush patrol in the jungles of the Nam. Each night on ambush each soldier would "pull guard" for three to five hours, depending on how many men were in each position. This did not allow room for much rest, but even when your time for sleep came, still you had to sleep with your boots on, ready to charge forward into battle at any moment.

Now, each night as soon as I get home, the first thing I do is take off my shoes, but I haven't forgotten that even this small freedom is mine because somewhere, even right now there are soldiers sleeping with their boots on, ready for battle. The hardships of a soldier are many, and included in the long list is being able to just lie down and rest without fear of loosing his or her life. Nights were long and difficult, and rest was nothing more than a myth or remembrance form a past way of life.

The time in the jungle sometimes passed quickly. On other occasions it seemed to move at the pace of a snail.

A bright spot in the midst of the darkness of being a soldier in harm's way came with re-supply when hopefully we would receive letters from home. This happened every four to six days, and was always a welcomed time.

I seldom had the opportunity to write home, but Glenda was faithful to write two or three letters each day. Even though they would all come at one time, I would read them according to the date, so I could see into her heart as she wrote each one. My hardship of being separated from home was terrible, but how much more so for my wife, not hearing from me for weeks at a time, and not knowing if I was alive or dead. The hardships of a soldier remain, even after the battles are fought, because even forty-six years later, I am still troubled at the thought of the anguish that Glenda experienced during those months of separation. The hardships of a soldier are shared with those he loves, and with those who love him.

From One Soldier To Another

1. What hardships are you facing right now?

2. What hardships are you facing that are the result of your standing in battle for the cause of Christ?

3. Will you see anew the Light that shines forth in the darkness and have your strength renewed, so as to endure hardships as a good soldier of the Lord?

A Soldier's Prayer

Gazing with spiritual eyes into the greatness of Your glory, Dear Father, I pray that hardships will come my way, because of my faithfulness to live a life of testimony to your love and grace in this day of battle. Until my bloody sandals and blood soaked garments are burned in the fire, help me to endure boldly awaiting that day. In the name of Jesus, I pray. Amen.

Chapter 4
The Horrors
of a Soldier

"So when this corruptible has put on incorruption, and this mortal has put on immortality, then shall be brought to pass the saying that is written: "Death is swallowed up in victory". O Death, where is your sting? O Hades, where is your victory?" The sting of death is sin, and the strength of sin is the law. But thanks be to God, who gives us the victory through our Lord, Jesus Christ. Therefore, my beloved brethren, be steadfast, immovable, always abounding in the work of the Lord, knowing that your labor is not in vain in the Lord." -- II Corinthians 15: 54-58... NKJV

Each soldier in his or her own way deals with the thought of dying on the battle field. Whether you talk about it or not, you know that in war there is always the possibility that you might be killed in action. For the combat soldier the risks are even higher, because of the engagement of the enemy face to face almost daily. In the heat of a "fire fight", the soldier does not have time to think about dying, just about trying to stay alive while at the same time eliminating the enemy.

Fighting always yields injury and sometimes death. Often when someone is killed, if he was not in you platoon, you might not know his name, and if you did know his name it would only be his last name. This served to help separate you from the death that so often surrounded you. Real names were often replaced with a nickname and this was how you were known.

Glenda sent me a lapel pin of Snoopy on his dog house, with his goggles on, and his scarf blowing in the breeze, which gave the impression that he was chasing that dreadful Red Baron. I put it through the camouflage cover of my helmet and bent the prongs on the back to secure it, and this caused me to gain the nickname "Snoopy", or as I was most often called, lovingly of course, "Snoop".

What is a name? Trying to remember names is difficult, but failing to remember the names of those who died is unforgivable. Sometimes it is difficult to remember their names. I'm so thankful that God doesn't forget our names.

"No one left behind", we lived by that code. No soldier, whether you knew his name or not would be left behind on the field of battle. One horror that a soldier faces each day is that of being left behind and taken POW, Prisoner Of War. During "Snake School" in those first few days "in country", I had the privilege to meet a former POW who had escaped after several months in captivity.

The information he shared by way of training, along with what I had already been taught, sealed the deal in my heart. I remember writing Glenda and telling her that if she received word that I was MIA, Missing In Action, don't believe it, I will not be taken alive. Even with this determined outlook, still each day there is the horror of being left behind.

In the early weeks of my tour, and after a few days on the point team, I was assigned to Lt. Kennedy as his RTO, Radio Tech Operator. After he was promoted and became company commander, his replacement, was a nice guy, but was straight out of OCS, Officer Cadet School, and he had obviously seen every John Wayne movie, because his desire for heroics interfered with common sense and good judgment. His decision process was different from mine, I think from most people.

Once, I remember, he sent me through a tree line and across a river bed to find a possible ambush site for the night. My common sense must have been on a break, because without thinking I did what I was told, like a good soldier, and found myself moments later separated from my unit which had moved on down the river.

The LT had forgotten about sending me across the river bed. His RTO separated and alone was inexcusable in military procedure, and in my procedure as well. For a moment anger overcame the horror of being separated from my platoon. Gathering my thoughts for a plan of action, I found a secure place with good visibility and waited for my gung-ho LT to realize that he needed me; for after all, I had the radio, and he would have to return to my location.

The greatest horror associated with combat is death; the death of a fellow soldier, or your own death. November 16, 1969 brought this very close to home for me. There had been a few men killed in our company prior to this day, but most of the time we worked in small units, with the platoon being the largest. Sometimes we set up in three or four man positions to make possible multiple ambush locations.

On this Sunday, we were moving as a platoon to set up multiple ambushes that night and serve as a blocking force for enemy activity. "Fonz", and he had this nickname long before TV came along with "Happy Days", had only five days left in country, and this was his last mission. It was my time to walk point, but Fonz wanted to walk point that day, his last time, and so I walked as his "slack". Thank the Lord, I had finally rid myself of that radio. We were moving down an old tank trail, which made for easy walking, but it also made a great place for "Charlie" to set up an ambush on us. We moved with caution all morning, and stopped for chow around noon.

Setting up in positions for security, the point team always had the forward responsibility, and we had a natural cover provided, a termite mound that was about five feet high and six feet across at the bottom. Those old mounds were as hard as concrete, so it would provide good cover. The other member of the point team that day was a man named Garcia, from New York, I think; he was the counter. You had to count your steps so you could determine where you were on the map, which was very important if you had to call in for artillery support. It had been a very quite morning and as we stopped for chow the only sound you could hear on this hot, dry day was the soft mumbling of soldiers as they ate. It was a good day in the jungle; no bullets, nobody dies.

We had just finished our delicious meal of our choice of the "C" ration entrée for the day, when Fonz decided to go to the position to our rear where Sgt. Crowe, Rabbit, and several others of our platoon were having noon chow, to get a light for a cigarette. Only a few meters away through the elephant grass, Fonz had to step high to walk down the thick foliage. Garcia and I were just relaxing, knowing that any minute we would be traveling again on this dry, hot day.

As Fonz was making his way back to us, retracing his steps, he hit a trip wire to a "boobie trap" which was located on the other side of the termite mound where Garcia and I were sitting. The explosion was so loud and the concussion was so great, it blew me forward three or four meters, but I landed with my rifle in my hand.

In the midst of the blast, as clear as day, I heard Fonz cry out, "Oh, my God". The next cry I heard was from my good buddy "Ears", Jerry Galant, who had come into Vietnam in the same group as I. Ears, my good friend, was hit, and he needed my help.

After securing the forward position and making sure this was not an incoming attack, I raced across the tank trail to check on my buddy, Ears, who was in extreme pain. He complained of the cans under his legs, thinking that his pack had been torn apart by the shrapnel from the explosion, but as I raised his legs to remove those cans, I discovered that the back of his legs had been blown away from the middle of his thighs down. He was covered with blood and bleeding. I took off my shirt and wrapped his legs as best I could to slow down his loss of blood. I helped to keep him comfortable, as best I could while our medic tried to work on his legs and the other seven men who were wounded.

Ears continued to bleed, blood was everywhere, on both of us. Ears had lost a lot of blood, and I wasn't sure he was going to live. This broke my heart. I knew that he might not walk again, even if he was able to survive this day. As he was placed on " medivac chopper" I knew I might not ever see Ears again. He spent many months in hospitals, and many long years getting to the place where he could walk again without the use of crutches.

Thirty eight years later, Ears located me and got my telephone number. The first time he called me was on November 16, the anniversary of the day he was wounded. He called to thank me for saving his life. He and I talk on the telephone from time to time. It is always good to hear his voice, and to know that he is doing well.

In 2009, Ears and I finally met again. He and his wife, Judy, met me in Louisville, Kentucky for lunch and a time to "catch up". This was a very emotional time for me, and very special. We shared what pictures we had of Vietnam, and just our thoughts of that terrible day, and what life has been like since. It was so good just to see Ears again, and to know that he is doing well, but that time together refreshed my mind to the vivid memories of that day, and the many days that followed.

Several of our men were wounded, some very seriously, but "Fonz" was killed. I looked down at him, and he was blown in half by the "boobie trap" that robbed him of his life that day, and every day thereafter. I remember Sgt. Sanders, our platoon sergeant, looked at me as we loaded him onto the chopper and said, "I don't think Fonz is going to make it". Fonz was dead, but even this veteran of war was in shock over seeing a comrade lay lifeless on the stretcher, and his mind would not accept the death of a friend. There are many horrors of war, but seeing a friend lying lifeless when only a few moments earlier you were talking about his going home, is one of the most difficult threats to sanity in a time of battle.

On this day, November 16, 1969, the war changed drastically for me. I had been a good soldier, always doing my best as I had been taught by my Dad. On this day, losing a friend, and seeing eight others wounded, this war was no longer just my duty, it became personal. I was not filled with hatred or wanting to seek revenge, I just became even more focused and intense on destroying as many enemy soldiers as I could.

While serving in the mountains of the Central Highlands in 1970, I lost another friend whose willingness to help others cost him his life. "Boxie", the title used by the Vietnamese for a doctor, was the medic of our platoon. I can't remember his real name; he was just "Boxie" to everybody. He had a great desire to help others and a great sense of humor. Often as we would pass through villages, and the local people would want this great American doctor to cure them of their ailments.

Salt tablets were pills that we would take to prevent dehydration, and Boxie had plenty of them. When we would pass through a village he would hand them out freely no matter what the sickness. It was amazing how many people he cured with those salt tablets. Doctors tell us that some sicknesses are a matter of the mind, and I guess that is true, or so it seemed to be. Still, Boxie liked to help others in need, no matter who they were.

Boxie was from Missouri, and was married with four children. He was twenty six years old and a conscientious objector. He should not have been in the field, but he was, and served valiantly tending to the physical needs of others.

On this particular day, we were assigned to a construction unit who was building a road through the mountains to a fire base located several clicks into the mountains of northern South Vietnam. This was good duty, because all we had to do was provide security while they worked, which meant not "humping" through the jungle with the one hundred and thirty five pounds of equipment on your back.

At night we would set up in ambushes hoping to catch "Charlie" unawares, and destroy an enemy that was determined to destroy us. At daylight, we would ride with the construction unit back into the mountains where they continued their work, and we would spend another day providing security for them. This was a dream mission for a grunt.

As we were making our way down the dirt road on this quiet morning with the dew still sparkling on the elephant grass, an explosion on the lead vehicle sent the hood flying into the air fifty or sixty feet. Riding on the back of a truck with several men, I turned to "Boxie" and said, "Boxie, we've got guys hurt up front". Just then another explosion ripped through the damp morning air throwing the second vehicle off of the road and rolling it across the ground. Again, I turned to "Boxie" and said, "Boxie, hurry up, they need you".

I was looking right at him when he jumped off of the truck and landed right on a mine which immediately threw him up in the air about thirty feet. It was as though his legs were made of springs as he so quickly was tossed up by the power of the explosion. I realized then that we were not receiving incoming rockets, but the road had been mined during the night. I commanded the rest of our men to jump as far from the truck as they could, staying away from the mines on the road.

After securing the area, attending to our wounded, and digging some shrapnel from my hand and the side of my head, I looked over at "Boxie". His torso was missing from the waist down, both legs and both arms were gone, and the back of his head looked as though it had been sliced away. Even in the drizzling rain that had just begun, he didn't bleed a drop.

I covered him with his poncho, and with a fellow soldier, Smithy, I began to look for the rest of his body. After searching for some time, all I found was his right hand and wrist and a small piece of one of his boots. I put the hand in my pocket and continued to search for more of Boxie. I placed the hand reverently under the poncho and stood there waiting for the chopper to come and pick him up.

Two hours passed waiting for the choppers to take in the wounded and then return for "Boxie", and I stood there in the now driving rain feeling nothing. I had seen so much injury and death, that there was a numbness of my heart. I cared, but I felt nothing. I wondered about "Boxie's" family, his wife and children, but I felt nothing. What had I become? Even an animal has feelings for those who die, but I felt nothing. The horror of battle had a strong grip on my heart, and I felt nothing.

There are many horrors of battle. The fears that grip your very existence can cause a person to react in ways he would not even consider under normal circumstances. The will to live, to survive, that God places in each heart, will drive us beyond what we think we can take. I am so thankful that God made us to withstand hardship and to stand in the safety of His grace and strength as we encounter the horrors of a soldier of the Lord, Jesus Christ.

FROM ONE SOLDIER TO ANOTHER

1. Life is full of joyous times, but the horrors of life are just as real, too. What are the horrors you are dealing with right now?

2. The horrors of living can eat away at the fabric of your soul, unless you rely on the help and strength of the Lord. Will you surrender your horrors to God?

3. The horrors of your heart are probably shared with those you love. Will you receive the rest that only our Lord can give, and in turn help those you love with their horrors?

A SOLDIER'S PRAYER

Dear Heavenly Father, You know the deepest hurts and the deepest desires of my heart, give me Your power to win the victory over the horrors of life. Help me to face the horror of death with the assured victory that comes from knowing Jesus as my personal Lord and Savior, for victory is mine, in Christ. Amen.

CHAPTER 5

THE HOPE
OF A SOLDIER

"Blessed be the God and Father of our Lord Jesus Christ, who according to His abundant mercy has begotten us again to a living hope through the resurrection of Jesus Christ from the dead, to an inheritance incorruptible and undefiled and that does not fade away, reserved in heaven for you, who are kept by the power of God through faith for salvation ready to be revealed in the last time."

-- I Peter 1: 3-5NKJV

Being a soldier in the jungles of Vietnam caused you to hope for many things when your mind was allowed a moment to just search the future. At night, during the dry season when the sky would be crystal clear, I would wonder what Glenda was thinking right then. You tried so hard to sleep, knowing that any moment you might be called into action, but often I would try to steal away a few moments just to imagine what the days would be like when and if I returned home to Glenda. Rest did not come easy, and sometimes you would be so tired that you just couldn't sleep. On those nights many thoughts or hopes would race through my mind giving me a brief escape from the dreadfulness of the horrors of war.

Thinking back to those nights when I was longing for a better day, I realize that it was moments like that which kept my heart strong and determined to survive no matter what. Even though death was all about me, still deep down inside I believed that one day I would return home to my darling wife, Glenda. Yet, there was a part of me that was so afraid that I would not survive this war, and that I would never see home again and know life as it had once been. One thing was certain, life would never be as it once had been, because the time in the jungle had changed life as I knew it. The definition of life had a new meaning now, and I wasn't even sure I knew what it was, but I sure hoped for the chance to learn.

When Peter wrote about a "living hope", exactly what did he mean? While I was a soldier in those jungles of Southeast Asia, I was a Christian and had been most of my life, but what exactly is this "living hope"? Oh, I knew the answer I was supposed to give when asked this question at church, but now when life all of a sudden has a new and deeper meaning and the challenges I faced each and every day were dealing with life and death, what is this "living hope"?

How wonderful it is to know that even when we don't know the right answers, God provides all we need to not only survive in the daily battles of life, but God gives that which we need to thrive in the battles of life. Jesus is the "Living Hope" in my life, and knowing Him as my personal Lord and Savior allowed me to be strong and courageous even when faced with death and difficulty.

I was no different than any other soldier when it came to "hope". I hoped I would live, I hoped I would one day go home with all of my limbs, I hoped Glenda's love for me would never end, and I hoped to live a really long life with her, having children and grandchildren. All of this seemed to crowd its way into my mind, and for a few seconds the dreadful moments of war would seem far away. It was that "hope" that made possible the brief escape for the reality of war, and strengthened my heart for the days of difficulty that lay ahead.

Looking into the darkness of the night sky, sometimes I would see a "freedom bird" flying over, filled with soldiers who had finished their time in Vietnam and were getting so close to all their hopes and dreams back in the "real world". I often would envy them, and wonder if I would ever be on one of those jets with some other soldier looking up and envying me. It was a hope that seemed so very far from my reach.

One night before I fell asleep and was just beginning my moment of "hope", one of our positions "popped the bush", exploded the claymore mines and opened fire on enemy that was to my right. All of a sudden this seemingly peaceful night exploded into gun fire and screams of agony. We were in a fire fight with several Viet Cong, who were surprised by our ambush, but still managed to put up a good fight. The battle was very intense and Lt. Kennedy called in a gunship, a helicopter with mini-guns mounted on each side, to help us in this battle. The empty casings from the gunship fell on our position like a hard rain, and in a matter of moments there was silence. Another battle had ended just as quickly as it had begun.

Now it was time to sweep the battle field and get that all important body count. The leaders in the "rear" had to know exactly how many enemy soldiers we had killed. As we swept across the small opening in the jungle and as I stepped across a log, Lt. Kennedy said, "Snoop, there's a great souvenir for you". I looked under the log and saw the two legs of an enemy soldier blown off from the knees down wearing some "home-made" Ho Chi Minh sandals still strapped on and covered with his blood.

I just stood there for a moment trying to absorb what I was looking at, and then without any feeling at all, I pulled those legs out from under that log and removed the scandals, and tossed the legs to the ground with no thought or feeling. Later I would send them home, and today they are on the bookshelf in my study, with dried mud and blood still there as a reminder of that battle long ago.

The enemy soldier had managed to drag his body

into a swamp where we lost the blood trail. I know he died, because nobody could loose that much blood and survive without medical attention. His hope for a better tomorrow was gone. This kind of subtle reminder caused me to reexamine my "hope list", and to have a greater appreciation for the wonderful gift of life.

Even after forty six years I can still remember those nights on ambush, the fire fights that were covered with blankets of darkness, but interrupted by the flashes of muzzles aimed to destroy the hope of an enemy, another living soul with hope. When the fighting stopped, there was that silent reminder that someone's hope had been taken away. Hope lost and gone forever.

The hope of life is not just about holding on and defending this wonderful gift of life that God gives to each of us, but there is a hope that is eternal which belongs to each person who will place their faith and trust in Jesus Christ. Strange as it seems to me now, I cannot remember ever thinking about the eternal destination of any of those enemy soldiers we faced in battle. They were the enemy and it was our job to kill them, and that is what we did.

Most of the Viet Cong were Buddhists, if they had any religion at all. They were very superstitious and feared the demons of the night. I never have understood how anyone could be absorbed by the false religions, but so many are, and they live without any hope at all. Outside of Jesus, there is no hope.

I am a Christian, and I was while serving my country in the jungles of Vietnam, but there were times when not even the knowledge and assurance of my eternal hope was enough to excite me about the gift of live in the drudgery of difficult days and nights. Deep in my heart I knew I was saved and that if I died I would go to heaven, but that wasn't enough to drive my heart to be thankful for the precious gift of life.

How easy it is for us to forget that Jesus died on the cross of Calvary just so we could be saved, know we are saved, and live in the joy of that salvation. How dare we waste one moment of basking in that blessed assurance. So many times I sought sleep on those many dreary nights without even a simple "thanks" to my Heavenly Father.

How thankful I am that the hope that Peter is writing about is not dependent on my keeping it safe and sure. Just as the song says, "My hope is built on nothing less than Jesus' blood and righteousness". It isn't about my ability to guard my hope, but it is all about the marvelous grace of the Lord that keeps that hope reserved for me in the strong grip of His hands.

FROM ONE SOLDIER TO ANOTHER

1. In what have you placed your hope?

2. If your life should suddenly come to an end in the next few moments, what hope do you have in eternity?

3. If you are a Christian, are you living life victoriously because you are assured of a certain hope in the eternal kingdom of God?

A SOLDIER'S PRAYER

Gracious Heavenly Father, Who is the Keeper of our eternal hope, help us to live each moment of each day in the joy of the hope that is reserved for us in Your glorious heaven. May Your love for us and our love for You be easily witnessed by the lost and dying world, and may our testimony of Your grace draw others to seek and find this blessed hope that is Jesus. Amen.

CHAPTER 6

THE HELP
OF A SOLDIER

"The Lord is my light and my salvation; whom shall I fear? The Lord is the strength of my life; of whom shall I be afraid? When the wicked came against me to eat up my flesh, my enemies and foes, they stumbled and fell. Though an army may encamp against me, my heart shall not fear; though war should rise against me, in this I will be confident. One thing I have desired of the Lord, That will I seek: That I may dwell in the house of the Lord All the days of my life, to behold the beauty of the Lord , And to inquire in His temple. For in the time of trouble He shall hide me in His pavilion; in the secret place of His tabernacle He shall hide me; He shall set me high upon a rock. And now my head shall be lifted up above my enemies all around me; therefore I will offer sacrifices of joy in His tabernacle; I will sing, yes, I will

sing praises to the Lord. Hear, O Lord when I cry with my voice! Have mercy also upon me, and answer me. When You said, "Seek My face," My heart said to You, "Your face, Lord, I will seek." Do not hide Your face from me; Do not turn Your servant away in anger; You have been my help; Do not leave me nor forsake me, O God of my salvation. When my father and my mother forsake me, Then the Lord will take care of me. Teach me Your way, O Lord, and lead me in a smooth path, because of my enemies. Do not deliver me to the will of my adversaries; for false witnesses have risen against me, and such as breathe out violence. I would have lost heart, unless I had believed that I would see the goodness of the Lord In the land of the living. Wait on the Lord; be of good courage, And He shall strengthen your heart; Wait, I say, on the Lord!"

-- Psalm 27: 1-14 NKJV

Help is something that we all need from time to time. We like to think we can do all things on our own, but the truth of the matter is, we need one another, and we most definitely need the Lord's help. When the psalmist was writing this Scripture text, he was revealing his need for the help of the Lord in his life. His dependence on the Lord for help in time of great struggle is obvious. His enemies seemed to have the advantage, and his end seemed to be one of doom. In wisdom he cried out to the only One who could help, the Lord, and the Lord saved him.

Soldiers are well trained and well equipped to handle almost any situation they may face. No matter the odds, because of the intense training and the confidence in the equipment issued, soldiers have an attitude that leads them into any battle, and with an assurance that the victory will be won. It may border on cockiness, but it is really a confidence in the ability to overcome, no matter the odds. Soldiers are determined to win, no matter the cost or sacrifice required.

A day in the life of the "bush soldier" in Vietnam was sometimes exciting, but often times so routine that you were tempted to let your guard down. When you are so tired, you get an attitude that you just don't care if you live or die. This is dangerous to you as a soldier, but it also puts your fellow soldiers in jeopardy, too. The days were long, hot, and very difficult, even if you did not make contact with the enemy. Just being a jungle fighter, with all you own and all you need to survive on your back, made each day so miserable, that there were times when you almost wished to die to put an end to the difficulties of the moment.

All aspects of every soldier's training instill the concept of "teamwork" in the heart and mind. There are times when you may be called upon to fight alone, but even then you have the support of fellow soldiers either directly or indirectly. The truth of the matter is, whether in civilian life or the life of a soldier, we need one another to be successful, to be assured of winning the victory. Another truth is that we all need the help of the Lord, if we are to do more than just survive in this life. With the help of the Lord we can thrive in this precious gift of life.

One day in the early fall of 1969, we were picked

up by a "chopper" to be taken quickly to a place where the enemy had been spotted. The urgency required our making contact with them before they could evaporate into the thick, triple canopy jungle. I was the RTO for Lt. Kennedy, so along with all my gear I also had to carry the PRICK 25, the field radio. Not only the extra weight made this an unpopular job, but the antenna was a dead give-away that you would be close to a leader, a target for an enemy soldier. Not a highly sought after job, but one assigned, and one I was determined to do well.

Since you had the extra weight and bulkiness of the PRICK 25, the RTO always sat in the door of the chopper with feet resting on the skid. You would be the last one to get on and the first one to get off. This wasn't a bad thing because those choppers would draw enemy fire. There was no sneaking up on the enemy at a landing zone, so if there was enemy anywhere around they would show up to take shots at the choppers and the soldiers on the choppers. I'm just a country boy, but I figured out real quick that whether I had the radio or not I wanted to be the last one on the chopper and the first one off. All of my tour, each time I could, I sat in the door with my feet on the skid.

On this particular day we were being air-lifted to a place where the enemy had been spotted. We were to go in, make contact, destroy the enemy, and move on to another location for setting up ambush that night. We had our orders and the plan seemed simple enough. All that remained was the execution, and we could get the job done. This was a very good platoon of combat veterans, seasoned by multiple battles and victorious in each one. We were good, really good.

As we approached the landing zone, a light rain filled the air. The field where we were landing was covered with elephant grass sticking up out of the water. We assumed that the water was only knee deep or waist deep at the most. We could see the top of the elephant grass. However, we didn't know that this elephant grass was over seven feet high, not unusual, but not the normal either. I had my M-16 in one hand and my PRICK 25 receiver wrapped in plastic to keep it dry in the other hand. It would be a hot LZ, or landing zone. We would be receiving enemy fire.

Since I was sitting in the door, it was imperative that I jump off the chopper quickly to make it safer for those who would follow me. As the chopper made the approach I stood on the skid and made my jump as we were three or four feet off of the water and elephant grass. The water was not knee deep, nor was it waist deep -- It was over seven feet deep! I jumped and landed surprisingly completely under water with my rucksack of one hundred and thirty five pounds and the PRICK 25 to make sure I stayed on the ground. My training demanded that as the RTO it was my job to make sure the radio was always in operation. On a rainy day like this that meant keeping the receiver dry, thus the plastic wrapped around it fastened with a rubber band. Instinctively I held the receiver as high as I could over my head to lift it out of the water and keep it dry.

In those moments, I knew I was about to die when suddenly I felt a strong hand grasp my wrist and pulling me up. As I broke out of the water I saw Lt. Kennedy holding my wrist. The chopper moved forward a few meters and I was able to rest my feet on the ground, still in the water, but only waist deep. All of this happened in a matter of a few seconds while we were receiving enemy fire. Lt. Kennedy had saved my life.

After we were all safely on the ground and had fought our way to dry ground, Lt. Kennedy smiled and said, "Snoop, your training saved your life. Like a good soldier you held that receiver up out of the water. It was the only thing I could see, that's why I was able to grab you by the wrist". Training, trying to be a good soldier, had saved my life, but we all need help from time to time.

No soldier ever really performs on his own, alone; it's always a team effort. We need the help of one another. This is a life lesson I've learned and been reminded of over and over. We are not here alone. We need the help of others. We need the help of God, our strong Commander, who grabs us from the depth of death and lifts us up to safety. It is the LORD who saves us from our sins, from ourselves. God pulls us out of our sinful circumstances and places our feet on the solid ground of His faithful salvation. Jesus is that salvation, and we can know for certain that we are safe and secure in Jesus.

From One Soldier To Another

1. How have you needed help in the last few days?

2. From whom did you first seek help?

3. As a Christian, we can be assured that help is available for every circumstance. We rely on the help of our Lord and Savior, Jesus Christ.

A Soldier's Prayer

Gracious, LORD, and Heavenly Father, how great and marvelous are Your ways, how great and glorious is Your Name. We realize that our help in all our trials comes from You. We acknowledge that we need You in every aspect of our lives. Cause us to faithfully look to You for the help we need just to live a life that is pleasing to You. Amen.

CHAPTER 7

THE HONOR
OF A SOLDIER

"For I know that this will turn out for my deliverance through your prayer and the supply of the Spirit of Jesus Christ, according to my earnest expectation and hope that in nothing I shall be ashamed, but with all boldness, as always, so now also Christ will be magnified in my body, whether by life or by death".
-- Philippians 1: 19-21 NKJV

Every soldier goes into battle with several thoughts going through his mind. There is the desire to be a good soldier, because of all the intense training you have endured. You want to do well, but you also want to live. However, there is something about a soldier that will cause him to act in a way that would not seem normal to others. There is that desire to do well, but it's more than just doing well, more than just being successful, more than just winning, more than just living. A real soldier wants to fight with honor, whether in living or dying, to fight with honor.

It was January 6, 1970, in the Central Highlands, I'm not sure exactly where we were. I was a squad leader, carrying the M 60 machine gun. I had two new guys who were my ammo mules. My mules carried two cans of ammo each for my M 60. I had a one hundred round starter belt, and when we made contact, my number one mule was to fall by my side and connect his ammo to my starter belt. The M 60 was the most powerful weapon we carried in the jungle, an amazing weapon.

Coming out of our nightly ambush before daybreak we moved to a location where we were joined by the other platoons and were resupplied there as a company of about eighty to one hundred men. We were moving to a specific location to be a blocking force for a large North Vietnamese element, number unknown. My squad had the rear as we moved single file through the hot and muggy jungle. It was going to be a long day. Being last in the formation, there was a lot of standing around waiting for the point team to slowly and safely make their way down this already worn trail.

Around midmorning, as I and my two ammo mules were waiting for the soldiers in front of us to move, I felt something hit my left shoulder. I had my M 60 resting on my right shoulder leaving my left exposed. Looking to the ground I saw a bamboo viper, a three step viper as they were called, lying by my foot. I crushed his head with the heel of my boot. The reason for being called a three step viper is that was about all the time you had to get the medicine in you to keep from dying. If that snake had landed on my ruck sack and bit me in the neck, I would have died in just a few minutes. With the dead snake at my feet, I smiled and thought, this is going to be a good day.

As soon as that thought crossed my mind, suddenly the point team was taking heavy enemy fire. Training kicked in, and I turned around and secured the rear of the formation just in case we were attacked from the rear as well. The fire fight continued for several minutes. It was obvious that we had encountered a larger than usual enemy element, but nobody expected a three day battle with a division. We received word that each of the point team was wounded and or dead. The fire fight continued trying to secure the place where the point team members were lying. After about an hour or so of intense exchanges of fire, the area where the point team was down was secured, and there was a temporary cease fire.

The point team was treated in the field and "dust off" choppers were called to fly the wounded out. Because of the triple canopy jungle they had to be lifted through the trees, but finally all the wounded were taken care of and thoughts were given to pursuing the enemy. All M 60 machine gunners and their mules were called to the front, including me and my squad. The plan, we were to sweep on line with M 60 at the ready fire position to look for the enemy. Because of the immense fire power the M 60 produced, we were walking on line to search out and kill the enemy that had attacked and wounded our friends.

I found myself walking on a well-worn path, with my M 60 at my side, ready to kill, and my two ammo mules walking behind me. Howard, from North Carolina, another M 60 squad leader, was to my right with his two ammo mules behind him. We stopped at the same time, looked at one another, the quietness was horrifying. I asked as softly as I could if he could hear or see any of our guys to his right? He answered no, and I answered the same concerning any of our guys to my left. We were out front of everybody else, all alone. I told him we should wait for the others to catch up, and he agreed.

On the trail in front of me was a log resting about twelve inches off of the ground. I decided I would kneel here and motioned to my ammo mules to take a knee. Even before I could rest my M 60 on that log, it seemed the world was exploding and coming to an end. Before I could fall to the ground I was hit in my right side with a round that just grazed me. In fact, I wasn't even aware that I had been shot until later. It wasn't bad, not when you consider men were wounded much worse and died that day. I dressed the wound myself. Only my ammo mules knew. I didn't allow myself to be turned in for a purple heart, it just didn't seem right. Three times I was wounded in combat. Each time men had died. It just didn't seem right for me to get the same medal others were getting, who had been wounded worse than I or killed, so I never mentioned my wounds to anybody.

The world was exploding right before my eyes. One round from an enemy rifle grazed and ricocheted across my M 60. Shrapnel was flying all over the place, because the enemy soldiers were throwing hand grenades and exploding claymore mines to our immediate front. Their suppressing fire was intense. I had been involved in many fire fights, but never had I experienced this, we were being over powered. I knew I was about to die, but I was determined I would not die easy and I would kill as many of them as I could before I died. As we were trained, Howard and I alternated fire, but we realized that wasn't going to work. We were cut off, we were over powered, and our soldiers from behind us had opened fire, putting us in a cross fire.

We were all about to die. Howard and I made eye contact for just a moment. We didn't speak. There was just that look affirming that death was certain. We opened fire, never letting up on the trigger. I would kill until my ammo was spent and then I would die. However, I was determined to kill as many as I could until I died. This was the plan.

My number two ammo mule had hooked up my starter belt from one of his cans, and I opened fire. I sprayed the area as much as I could. No three round bursts, but I was firing as much as I could, trying to cover as much area as I could, for as long as I could, as long as I would live. The more we fired, the more the enemy fired back at us. Still, we had no place to go, we continued to fire and fire and fire. After several thousand rounds and a fire fight that had lasted several minutes, there was a cease fire by the enemy. They had just stopped. We were trapped, we were running low on ammo, we are in a crossfire, we were doomed, and just as suddenly as the fight started, it ended.

I looked at Howard, he looked at me, each of us knowing we had cheated death, at least for the moment. I turned to my number one ammo mule and asked him if I still had my legs. In the heat of the battle, the way it started, and the intenseness of those minutes, I didn't know if my legs had been blown off or not. This was his first fire fight. He was already petrified, and he asked me "What did you say?" I asked him a second time, "Do I still have my legs?" He looked, and with a bewildered stare shook his head yes. I told him to crawl backwards; let's get out of here.

For several meters we crawled, until we thought it safe to stand and walk. By this time we had crawled back to where our guys were positioned. I put my M 60 on my right shoulder and was holding it by the bipod as we walked through our front line of soldiers to go back and regroup and resupply. The usually black barrel of my M 60 was white as snow because it was so hot, but it had not even jammed at all during that fire fight. That in itself was a miracle, but this was a day of miracles. As we walked through our soldiers to the rear, nobody said a word to us, they just stared. They were looking at dead men who had come back from death, yet we walked among the living.

I set my M 60 down to let the barrel cool, while I sat

down to try and calm down. My heart was still racing, the rush of combat, well, it's just beyond description by words of man. It was then I noticed I had been wounded, and I dressed the wound. I saw to it that my ammo mules were given two new cans each of ammo, because I was sure we would need it. We did, for three more days we fought in that same place. We would fight, advance, and then have to fall back, but each day gaining a little more ground, a little better position on the enemy.

At night, what little we were able to sleep, we were surrounded by charred timber from the air strikes, and the smell of burnt flesh from our enemy. That first night, I reflected on the events of that day. I thought about that log, and how it must have absorbed most of the bullets and shrapnel that had come my way. That log had saved my life, or so I thought. Three days later we had fought our way back to the place where Howard and I had been. I found myself standing at that same log, looking down at it, thinking how that log had saved my life.

As I put my foot on it to step over it, it crumbled about two feet in each direction. It was a termite infested log. It would not have stopped anything, it was mostly dust just gathered in the form of a log. It was then that I realized, my life was not saved by a log, but by the Lord, Himself. I should have died that day, I knew I was going to die that day, but God had other plans. Why God would save me on that day or any day still amazes me, but He did, and I will always be grateful. That God would save me for all eternity is even more amazing, but

He has, and for that I will be eternally grateful.

Howard and I killed seventeen enemy soldiers on that first day, defending ourselves and determined to kill as many enemy soldiers as we could before we died. We fought with honor. If I had died that day, I would still be grateful that God allowed me to live and die with honor. What more can a good soldier ask of his Commander. However, God had other plans for me. I still struggle with the fact that I lived and so many of my friends died. I struggle in that and live silently a life of apology in my heart.

To live with honor is not just the responsibility of a soldier in the army, but of every born again believer, every saved child of God. We may fail, I sin daily, but the determination of our heart should be to live with honor, to live in honor of our Lord and Savior, Jesus Christ. So may our lives be lived in honor.

ONE SOLDIER TO ANOTHER

1. How would you define honor?

2. What does it take for you to live a life that honors the Lord?

3. Whether we live or die, our life should always honor our Savior, Jesus.

A SOLDIER'S PRAYER

Gracious Lord, You have honored us in dying for us on Calvary's cross. You honor us each day by being our constant Protector and Provider. Help us to so live as to honor You in all that we do, and when time comes to die, may we honor You in that moment, too. Amen.

Chapter 8
The Home
Of A Soldier

"But you, O man of God, pursue righteousness, godliness, faith, love, patience, gentleness. Fight the good fight of faith, lay hold on eternal life, to which you were also called and have confessed the good confession in the presence of many witnesses. I urge you in the sight of God Who gives life to all things, and before Christ Jesus Who witnessed the good confession before Pontius Pilate, that you keep this commandment without spot, blameless until our Lord Jesus Christ's appearing, which He will manifest in His own time, He who is the blessed and only Potentate, the King of kings and Lord of lords, Who alone has immortality, dwelling in unapproachable light, Whom no man has seen or can see, to Whom be honor and everlasting power. Amen."

-- I Timothy 6: 11-12 NKJV

Each day in Vietnam was a challenge, and each day brought a new challenge. There was the heat, the rain, the dry, the heavy rucksack (back pack), the heat......did I mention the heat, and of course the fact that the VC were trying to kill you. Then there were the small but annoying things that are so easily taken for granted here in the United States. We are so blessed in this country that we have lost our sense of what is truly valuable and precious.

When I get home the first thing I do is to take off my shoes. Being a country boy at heart, I just love to go bare foot. This was a luxury not allowed in the jungle. We only removed our boots long enough to put on foot powder or medicine to fight the jungle rot, and we did this one at a time so we would never be caught off guard from an enemy attack. I almost lost three toes due to the excessive moisture in my boots that caused jungle rot. I have a scare on my shin where I had jungle rot, and it still scabs over two or three times a year.... forty-six years later and counting.

Water was so precious. During the rainy season there was always plenty of water. You could drink as much as you wanted, and then refill your canteens from the rain. We were allowed one canteen, one quart of water each day. I am still amazed at how we managed to stay hydrated. However, during the dry season when the heat was beating down on you, it was nothing more than what seemed to be a distant dream to have a cool drink of water.

I've always heard that you can only go three days

without water, but I know that isn't true. Once during the dry season we couldn't be resupplied on time because of receiving heavy enemy fire. I ran out of water and didn't have anything to drink for four days. It was miserable. At night it was so hot and I was so thirsty that I couldn't sleep. I would wish to just die and put an end to my suffering. I made myself a promise that if I lived to get back to the "real world" I would never allow myself to be thirsty again. Now, I hardly pass a water fountain without stopping to get a cool drink of water.

Many think that the home for a guerrilla fighter in Vietnam would be the triple canopy jungle where your time was spent hunting and being hunted. That would be an easy assumption, but home is not where you spend your time, it is where your heart is. So, with that being said the next response would be the "real world", the U.S.A. where friends and family were. However, for an infantry soldier, one whose only training is to kill and survive, home is combat. There is no substitute for the rush of adrenaline like you experience in a fire fight at close range.

My first contact with the enemy came quickly on my first day in the jungle, on a seeming quiet journey. The night's rain still lingered on all the vegetation. What part of you that wasn't wet from the leftover rain was wet because of the heat. As we made our way through the "bush", jungle, as quietly as possible, I was extremely cautious and observant. I knew the point man was relying on me to have his "six", his back, in case of contact with the enemy. You see, I was walking "slack", right behind the point man, a lot of soldiers were depending on me, a new guy, to do his job as well as anyone else.

Suddenly the quietness of morning was interrupted by enemy gun fire, coming at me. I had never been shot at before by somebody wanting to kill me. I am and never have been a violent person. All my life, so far, of sixty five years, I have never hit another person in anger. Before this moment, I had thought over and over in my mind wondering if I would react as I was supposed to, or would I freeze and cause my fellow soldiers to die. The answer to that question came quickly and without a thought. My training kicked in and as if I had been doing this all of my life, I responded by covering my point man and returning fire toward the enemy.

I could see the Viet Cong, but not see their faces, just that they were trying to kill us. I'm not sure how many enemy soldiers the point man and I killed, and I can't even remember the body count. It all happened so suddenly, lasted for what seemed like an eternity, and then just as suddenly as it began, it ended. The silence was deafening, the heat from my M-16 mixed with the dampness caused smoke to rise from my barrel. We lay there in stillness, waiting to see if we had eliminated all of the bad guys.

After assuring the safety of the rest of our platoon, the two of us moved forward very slowly making sure the danger was past. We found the dead bodies of the enemy, men who gave their lives trying to take ours. I looked at their faces, like me, they were young men, but now their life was over. There would be nothing left for them on this earth, but a burial hole as a final resting place. We took their weapons, looked in their pockets for any valuable information, turned in the body count, and then moved on. It was just another day in the Nam. It didn't mean anything.

I had a few minutes to gather my thoughts before we moved out. I was pleased that I had responded as a good soldier and was told that by Lt. Kennedy. In combat, my first combat, I had done well. I was relieved and proud that I had fought as a good soldier. As hard as it is for those who have never had the privilege of serving our great country in the line of fire, I knew this was what I was trained to do. The sense of purpose and accomplishment was so rewarding. I was perfectly at home being engaged in combat. It's not that I loved killing so much as it was having the pride to know I was removing bad people who were doing really bad things to innocent people. I was helping the less fortunate and defending the right of freedom for those who could not defend themselves.

A few days later our platoon came back together from squad sized ambush sites to move to a new area of operation. Once we would get there, we would break down into squad size and set up multiple ambush sites to prevent enemy movement. These locations were determined by Army Intelligence somewhere in a room with maps and radios. These folks moved the grunt, jungle fighter, around like chess pieces.

As we were moving to this new location the point team was ambushed by a few Viet Cong. The point team was killed. Three American soldiers lost their life in the matter of a few seconds. Lt. Kennedy responded by directing our movement to engage these killers. As we moved out, I once again found myself in the point team. I wasn't a super soldier, I just did my job well, and even though I had been in the "bush" for only a few days, I was trusted. I just always tried to do my best, I still do.

We engaged the enemy, and this time we were not caught by surprise, but surprised them and killed them, every one. Lt. Kennedy left a squad with the killed and injured and the rest of us moved out in hot pursuit. That is why we surprised them. They thought we would huddle, lick our wounds, and so we caught them off guard. I remember standing there with one of the dead enemy soldiers lying at my feet, when one of our soldiers ran up and in frustration shot the dead enemy soldier three times.

The three men in our point team that were killed were strangers to me, I didn't even know their names, but they were brothers in battle. "Gook", I don't remember his real name, was from West Virginia, and he is the one who was expressing his anger and shot the dead VC at my feet. I just watched, I had no feeling of my own, except for anger. There are a lot of emotions that you experience in combat. I believe that every emotion, every sense, all reach a peak as the rush of combat confronts you. Fear and the other emotions are turned into a strength that allows you to do what seems impossible, it enables you to be the best soldier in combat, an

American soldier.

Even after all these years have passed by, there has never been one day to go by without me thinking about Vietnam and combat. I still miss combat. It isn't the idea of taking a life, but that of defending our freedom and helping people who are being oppressed by those filled with hatred. As long as there are people on earth there will be wars and rumors of war, the Bible tells us that very plainly. There are always those who are filled with evil to the point that they will take whatever others have, all that is valuable, including their lives.

In the heart of a soldier burns the desire for combat, to do that which is right, and to be a help to others. It's all about taking care of your fellow man, and about being a guardian of justice, decency, and the love of life. So it is even truer for Christians, those who are soldiers of the LORD Jesus Christ, as Paul reminds Timothy in I Timothy 6:11-12. We are to "fight the good fight of faith, and lay hold on eternal life". From life experience as a soldier in the jungles of Vietnam, and as a soldier of the LORD since I was just a boy, you will not fight the good fight, unless you know combat as the home of a soldier.

ONE SOLDIER TO ANOTHER

1. There is an old saying, "home is where the heart is". Where is your heart?

2. For what are you willing to die? Will you give you heart, your passion to live for Jesus?

3. Home is a place of safety and comfort, a place to be defended. Will you defend your home no matter the cost?

A SOLDIER'S PRAYER

Our Heavenly Father, the Giver of life, the Sustainer of life, the Provider of life eternal through Your Son and our Savior, Jesus Christ. Thank You for giving us an assured home in glory by Your saving grace. Until the time You call us home for eternity may we fight the good fight as a good soldier of Jesus Christ. Help us to be true and faithful and a defender of the home You put in our care. Amen.

Chapter 9

The Hurt
Of a Soldier

"Do not fret because of evildoers, Nor be envious of the workers of iniquity. For they shall soon be cut down like the grass, And wither as the green herb. Trust in the Lord and do good; Dwell in the land, and feed on His faithfulness. Delight yourself also in the Lord, And He shall give you the desires of your heart. Commit your way to the Lord Trust also in Him, And He shall bring it to pass. He shall bring forth your righteousness as the light, And your justice as the noonday. Rest in the Lord, and wait patiently for Him;"

-- Psalms 37: 1-7 NKJV

In every close knit group of people when one person is hurt it has a dramatic effect on the entire body.

These words could not be truer when speaking about the United States Military. No matter what branch of the service a person belongs to, hurting one is to hurt all. This is a brotherhood of soldiers who live and fight and die together and who have a bond that goes beyond the imagination of most people. This is so true of the men and women who served valiantly in Vietnam.

A few years ago my wife and I had the privilege to travel to Washington D. C. where we were able to visit the different war memorials and Arlington Cemetery. I cannot put into words how much that trip meant to me, and it still does today. I will never forget the first time I saw the Vietnam Memorial.....The Wall. I couldn't speak and if I could have, I had no words to say, just a heart filled with emotion.

I stood there, just off of the grounds, just staring at The Wall for what seemed like an hour or so, but I'm sure it was only a few minutes. My legs would not move to go near this magnificent monument of honor. Tears streamed down my face while in my chest my heart was being broken in a thousand pieces. There were many people there walking around, but I could only see The Wall as I stood like a statue. Several detailed thoughts raced through my mind, all involving combat and death. My emotions were in warp speed, but at the same time had the pace of a snail with nowhere particular to go.

Glenda told me she would wait and sit on the bench under the shade of a tree and give me as much time as I wanted to just be near The Wall, alone. She told me to look around and she would make my picture. I refused......no pictures. To me this was a very sacred place, not a tourist attraction. It upset me to see most of the people talking, laughing, and making pictures in just random stops along The Wall.....just a picture, meaning nothing to them....just a picture.

The loud talking, laughter, and chatter were just too much for me, so I made my way along The Wall only occasionally stopping to just stare at the names, none of which I knew. Getting back to where Glenda was seated on the bench, I told her I would wait and let the crowd get smaller and I would go back then.

The crowd didn't get smaller. There was just this continuous throng of people making their way along The Wall. Some had notes and were looking for specific panels to locate the name of a loved one. Some would place a piece of paper over the selected name and rub a pencil over it making the engraving in the stone appear on the paper. I went to the large, thick record books placed near The Wall. I searched through the book looking up names of men I knew who had died in Vietnam and writing down their panel location. Then I returned to the wall just to find the name, see the name, and trace the name with my index finger. As I remembered how each one died so vividly in my mind, tears poured down my cheeks. I don't cry in front of people. I am a very strong man. Now, I didn't care who saw me.

Then I remembered one other soldier who I watched die, one who was a very close friend to me, Boxie, a medic, a conscientious objector. He carried no weapon but served deep in the jungle with us, taking care of us.

The day he was killed shook my soul. I will never forget the events of that day. Now, as I returned to the record book, I realized that I didn't know his name, just his nickname, Boxie. I do not have the words to describe how helpless and hopeless I felt at that moment. I was so frustrated. How could I not know his real name, but I didn't. There was no way to retrieve his name or location on The Wall. I walked away.

I'm not sure visiting all the war memorials, especially The Wall, and Arlington Cemetery is on the recommended list for those suffering with PTSD, but the opportunity to do so is a life event that I will never forget. I've been to many National Cemeteries and served as a part of an honor guard for many military funerals, but walking through Arlington is very special. For the most part there was silence and reverence there. Glenda and I did not join a tour group, just got a map and walked and looked at our own pace. It was quieter.

We took it all in, from the changing of the guard at the tomb of the Unknown Soldier to finding some graves of many heroes of days gone by. The time passed quickly and the time to leave brought with it mixed emotions. I could have stayed longer. It seemed to be so peaceful there. Even though each grave marker was a reminder of a fallen soldier, still this was the final resting place of men and women who gave their lives for the freedom we enjoy and so often take for granted. I felt right at home there, even though it hurt.

The hurt of a soldier comes in many forms. It can happen when you leave home and loved ones behind.

That's always difficult. I remember the tears and the look in the eyes of friends and family, not knowing if we would ever see each other again. The unknown can cause a great deal of stress and bring with it a pain for which there is no medicine.

Hurt can happen during training as your body and mind are being forced to make adjustments from civilian life to the Army way. Of course leadership is provided to help you in this time of challenge. Drill sergeants have a way of seeing to it that the trainee continues no matter the pain and hurt. I remember the every Friday P.T. test and the low crawl on that long tarp. All of the skin was worn off of my chest and it never had a time to heal until I left basic training. It hurt, a lot.

Certainly in combat each soldier experiences hurt. I was wounded three times but was never given a purple heart. I dressed my wounds and continued to fight. Each wound was very painful and one took an exceptionally long time to heal. The scar only disappeared a few years ago. For the soldier in combat hurt comes whether you are wounded or not. You hurt when your brothers in arms hurt. You hurt when a fellow soldier dies. You hurt just being there, hunting and being hunted. You hurt from fatigue that leads you to the place when you don't care if you live or die.

As a Christian, you know to patiently wait on the LORD for His healing touch, but this is so hard to do when your mind and body ache because of the hurt of combat and the labor of just living another day in Vietnam. There are times when the mental hurt and fatigue is so severe that you wish to die. At least death would bring some relief from the hurt you experience each day. When a soldier gets to the place when he doesn't care if he lives or dies.....this is a very dangerous place.

Arriving home, back to the United States of America, does not end the hurt. You would think that to return home alive would put an end to all the hurt, all the pain.....you would think. Unfortunately this is not true. No war has been as unsupported as the Vietnam war, and no soldiers have been so disrespected as the Vietnam veterans. Coming home was not an end to the hurt, but rather a new hurt, one even more painful than hot shrapnel burning into your body. The stares and the whispers pierced deeply into the hearts of soldiers as we returned home. A new pain like no other.

FROM ONE SOLDIER TO ANOTHER

1. All of us experience hurt in this life. How are you hurting, right now?

2. Your hurt may not have scars that show, but the hurt is very real. From where did your hurt come?

3. Right now, will you give that hurt to God and trust Him to give you healing?

A SOLDIER'S PRAYER

Our gracious LORD and Heavenly Father, we hurt. We confess that we can do nothing to ease the pain. All of our attempts to remove the pain has only caused frustration and doubt. Please, help us to place our trust in Your healing touch. Give us the satisfaction of knowing that You care for us and that Your care is sufficient to meet all our needs, and mend all our hurts. To You we look for the strength to face each new day. In Jesus holy and precious name we pray. Amen.

CHAPTER 10

THE HEALING
OF A SOLDIER

"God is our refuge and strength, a very present help in trouble. Therefore will not we fear, though the earth be removed, and though the mountains be carried into the midst of the sea; Though the waters thereof roar and be troubled, though the mountains shake with the swelling thereof. Selah. There is a river, the streams whereof shall make glad the city of God, the holy place of the tabernacles of the most High. God is in the midst of her; she shall not be moved: God shall help her, and that right early. The heathen raged, the kingdoms were moved: he uttered his voice, the earth melted. The Lord of hosts is with us; the God of Jacob is our refuge. Selah. Come, behold the works of the Lord, what desolations he hath made in the earth. He makes wars to cease unto the end of the earth; he breaks the bow, and cuts the spear in sunder; he burns the chariot in the fire. 10 Be still, and know that I am God: I will be ex-

alted among the heathen, I will be exalted in the earth. The Lord of hosts is with us; the God of Jacob is our refuge. Selah."
-- Psalm 46:1-11 NKJV

Part of life, unfortunately, is hurt and pain and the need to heal. Every soldier, in every war, has been hurt, suffered pain and has a need to heal. Coming home from combat does not heal the wounds of the heart for a soldier. Actually for the combat soldier, home, the place where you feel the most comfortable, is engaging the enemy. This doesn't mean you are a lover of war, but this is what you are trained to do. Nothing is more satisfying than doing that which you are prepared to do, and doing it very well.

I was trained to kill and survive, and I did my job very well. I was not a "Rambo" soldier, just a very good soldier. I am forty five years plus removed from Vietnam and combat. There has never been a day, not one day that I have not thought about the jungle and there has not been one day, not one day that I haven't missed and longed for the opportunity to engage an enemy, to put my life on the line for my country, and to defend those who cannot defend themselves. Maybe I'm not normal, I don't know. This I do know, I left a part of me in the jungles of Vietnam, and I brought another part of Vietnam home with me.

As just one of millions of soldiers who have fought in a war and who suffer with Post Traumatic Stress Disorder, or PTSD, the scars never go away and the pain continues. There is no complete healing. With God's help I manage to continue a very productive life, but only in His strength. However, there are some things in life that are not taken away until death. The memories of Vietnam still haunt me each night. I do not even remember when I last had a good night's sleep without the horror of the dreams that seem so real.

When I first returned home from Vietnam, I was assigned to Fort Hood, Texas, where I would finish my active duty career. State side duty was very difficult for me. I was sent to the only infantry battalion on the base. Out of all the mechanized units, I get attached to another infantry unit. Again, boots on the ground. When I reported to headquarters, Top, the Sargent Major decided to help out an old tired grunt. He asked me if I had a military license, to which I replied "no". He asked me if I thought I could drive a "duce and a half", a two and a half ton truck, which seemed immediately better than walking, so I said I was sure I could.

Top sent me to the drivers' license division to get my big truck driver's license. As I got there, I saw all the big trucks, buses, and other vehicles parked, and all the cones in place for driving tests. I was certain I could never fake my way through any of those obstacles. The instructor had me fill out all the necessary paperwork and took me to a single chair with two pedals in front of it and two lights on the dashboard behind the steering wheel. He had me put my right foot on the left pedal and watch the green light. I was instructed as soon as I saw the green light go off and the red light come on, I was to remove my right foot from the right pedal and as quickly as I could press down on the left pedal. This was a reflex test I just knew I could do. The lights changed and I changed pedals with my foot as quickly as I could. The instructor said, "Well, Harrison, you passed. Take this paper to the desk and get your license". I couldn't believe it. That's all I had to do. I was good to go. I could learn to drive a big truck, and I did.

I soon found out that state side duty was very different than what I had been used to in my daily life. During basic training and advanced infantry training there was the constant pressure to hurry up, learn, execute, and get ready for what is next. In Vietnam, each day in the jungle was the same, yet different. We would move out at sunrise or earlier and hunt for the enemy all day long. We were moving toward the next ambush position that was determined by headquarters based on Army intelligence. We would set up the ambush at dusk or right after and wait for unsuspecting enemy soldiers to come into our kill zone and we would terminate them.

This was what my days in the jungles of Viet Nam were like.....each day. You slept very little because of being on guard part of each night. You always had to be ready, that's why we slept with our boots on. Always ready to fight. You were always tired, always hot, always wet....with sweat during the dry season and soaked through and through during the monsoon season. You might say it was a very demanding and discouraging life. However, compared to the laid back agenda of state side duty which was so boring, at least you knew you had an extremely important task to do each second of each day in the jungle.

Coming home, I arrived at Fort Lewis, Washington at five minutes after midnight. We moved from the Flying Tiger Airlines jet to a large room where all of us stood. There were two hundred plus of us crowed into this room waiting to see what was next. A captain entered the room and told us that his responsibility was a debriefing or lecture that would help us as we were now in the "real world", the U.S.A. once again. He had an hour to tell us all about what we could expect. He walked to the podium and made this statement, "You are not going to fit into the "real world", so just deal with it". Then he just turned and walked out of the room. That was my briefing for reentry into the "real world". I couldn't believe it. Nothing to help, just deal with it. So I have tried to do that, but find it is very difficult to do.

From there we were bused to supply where we were measured for new dress greens uniforms, given personal hygiene essentials, and taken to a barracks where we could shower and try to get the stench of the jungle off of our bodies. It didn't work. No matter how hard you scrubbed or how many showers you took, still the jungle smell remained. When I got out of the shower my new dress greens were hanging there waiting for me. My name tag, rank, and medals were all in place. I was impressed, to say the least, at how the Army could make all this happen right on time. From there we were once again bused to the mess hall where we had T-bone steaks and eggs, since it was four in the morning. This was my first T-bone steak I had ever had. It tasted so good.

After breakfast I lined up to get travel pay, and then called the airlines to get a ticket home, or at least as close as I could get. That would be Memphis, Tennessee, the same place I had left from over a year ago. I remember the lady asked me if I wanted to fly military standby and save some money. I told her, "No thank you, I want a ticket, I'm going home". There was excitement as I called Glenda, after my flight was secured and gave her my arrival information. She was somewhat excited, too. The airport was getting quite busy as people were gathering for travel. I walked to my gate seemingly unnoticed. Nobody said a word to me. Most tried to avoid any eye contact at all. I sat in silence in a crowed airport, yet all alone. It was then I realized I was still hurting and there was no healing expected.

I arrived in Memphis at three in the afternoon and walked out of gate three to the smile and open arms of my wife, Glenda. She had come alone to meet me. We were not noticed as we hugged, laughed, and she cried tears of joy. There were no tears in my eyes. I was glad to be home, with her, but even in that moment I felt as if nobody cared and that I was not welcome because of the uniform I wore. After my time of active duty was ended, I just tried to blend into the day by day life that was expected of me. I remained silent about my days in combat, trying my best to just "cowboy up" and deal with the hurt and waiting on time to heal. Time doesn't heal anything, only God can heal.

After years and years and years of trying to handle the hurt and wait for the healing, I realized there are some things that require a great deal of time to heal. God's time. I am convinced that there are some things that God only heals when we leave this life for our home in heaven. As I write this chapter, all alone, tears stream down my face. I weep out loud. My hurt is almost unbearable, but I know that God has this, and that He will provide what I need each day. God's strength is my strength. God is my Refuge, my Hiding Place, and in Him I will trust and wait for Him to heal my hurt.

It has been over forty five years since I came home from Viet Nam. Each day is a new day with new challenges. Each night I dream and my mind races back to the jungles of Vietnam. I can't escape the dreams. As I grow older the dreams are more detailed than ever before. Now I see faces where once the enemy in my dreams were faceless. I see the anger and the fear in their faces. I feel the adrenaline rush of combat, my heart races, and my breath quickens. Every night I face the demons of my past. My hope for sanity in all this is the LORD, my God, my Savior, Jesus Christ. Even if healing comes at my death, I will trust in Jesus.

From One Soldier To Another

1. Life is filled with battles, but not all are on a battlefield. Hurts are the result of battle. What hurts do you have for which you need God's healing?

2. Healing requires time which means patience. Will you give God your hurts and wait for His divine healing in His divine timing?

3. A refuge is a place of safety even when the storms or battles still rage. A refuge will not end the storm or the battle, but is a secure resting place. Will you let Jesus be your Refuge?

A Soldier's Prayer

Gracious Heavenly Father, I confess my weaknesses, my inability to heal the hurts of the battles of this life. I have tried to handle my hurts in my own strength. I have failed. Give me refuge, strength, courage, and patience to wait upon You. I know that You and only You can heal the hurts of my heart. Please, heal me, and be my Refuge. I want to find rest in Your loving arms. I place my faith in You and depend on You for my help. In Jesus name I pray. Amen.

EPILOGUE:

I AM A SOLDIER OF JESUS CHRIST

"You therefore, my son, be strong in the grace that is in Christ Jesus. And the things that you have heard from me among many witnesses, commit these to faithful men who will be able to teach others also. You therefore must endure hardship as a good soldier of Jesus Christ. No one engaged in warfare entangles himself with the affairs of this life, that he may please Him who enlisted him as a soldier."
-- II Timothy 2: 1-4 NKJV

Now, as an old soldier looking back, I realize that the war in Vietnam was not the only battles of my life. As a pastor for almost thirty-seven years there are struggles and challenges as you try to be the best shepherd for

God's flock that you can be. It's not easy to please the flock when your desire is to please the Good Shepherd. However, if you stop to think about it, life, everyday life, is filled with challenges and struggles. Life isn't for sissies. I believe my personal motto for Vietnam, and for ministry, and for everyday life has an encouragement for each of us. "If you live to fight another day, it's been a good day". May you be blessed with many good days.

-- Dr. C. Wayne Harrison
"Snoopy"

You therefore, my son, be strong in the grace that is in Christ Jesus. And the things that you have heard from me among many witnesses, commit these to faithful men who will be able to teach others also. You therefore must endure hardship as a good soldier of Jesus Christ. No one engaged in warfare entangles himself with the affairs of this life, that he may please Him who enlisted him as a soldier." -- II Timothy 2: 1-4 NKJV

I AM A SOLDIER OF JESUS CHRIST

DR. C. WAYNE HARRISON

PUBLISHED *by*
PARABLES
Earthly Stories with a Heavenly Meaning